THE DAYS OF
DINKUM DODGER

VOLUME I

JOHN SAOMES

Copyright © John Saomes 2015

The right of John Saomes to be identified as the author of this work has been asserted in accordance with the Copyright, Designs and Patents Act, 1988. All rights reserved. No part of this book may be reproduced, stored in a retrieval system, or transmitted, in any form, or by any means, electronic, mechanical, photocopying, recording or otherwise, without the written permission of the publisher.

Inspire Point Publishing
PO Box 972
Beenleigh Queensland 4207
Australia
Email: admin@inspirepointpublishing.com

Cover Design - Peta Hansford
Illustrations - Kym Lui
Interior Design - Peta Hansford

The Days of Dinkum Dodger - Volume I
ISBN: 978-0-9942910-2-8

"I'm a big fan of Banjo Patterson and Henry Lawson with their quintessential Aussie flavoured bush ballads, and John Saomes hasn't disappointed with this witty collection of poems."

"Saomes shows throughout this collection he is adept at witty, solemn and endearing verse."

"These yarns strike a chord within the Australian spirit … the larrikinism of the decent fun-loving Aussie bloke jumps from every page."

"Pranks, accidents, local myths and legends, and political incorrectness, the fate of our society, and even a few yarns based on real events — full of good old Aussie slang. Even the scathing political poems have a splash of Aussie humour."

"A rollicking good read and excellent first volume of Dinkum Dodger's bush poetry."

"John Saomes's poetry celebrates the life of genuine Australians and makes me fiercely proud of my Australian heritage."

"A welcome return of the larrikin storyteller. These immortal yarns reflect the political opinion and social mores held dear by the majority of True Blue Australians. It would do well for politicians to be cognisant of this reality articulated so well."

Discover other titles by John Saomes at
www.johnsaomes.com

*This book is dedicated to that great
Aussie pioneering spirit,
the spirit that is fair dinkum,
true blue Australian.*

TABLE OF CONTENTS

Preface ix

PART I
LAUGHING MATTERS
    School Days 3
    Outhouse Blues 5
    Baking Day 10
    The Crooked Willy Wongle 14
    The Phantom Bell Ringer 17
    Drought In Bamaga 20
    The Legend Of The Itching Crutch 22
    A True Irish Elephant Story 27
    Before Fitzgerald 29
    Kanty's Hat 32
    Insurance Assurance 34
    Goanna Stew 37
    Sunday Morning Fracas 40
    Lurks And Perks 42
    My Salute To Dad 'n Dave 44

PART II
LIFE & POLITICS
    The Noble Art Of Recitation 49
    Political Persuasion 50

Darcy's Daybreak	53
Government Controls	54
Dangerous Games	56
Thoughts Of The Night	57
Land Rights	58
The Long Yard Of Anticipation	59
The Wuzzle's Tale	60
We Need A First Amendment	63
Ode To The Dunstans	65
What Are You Teaching	68
World Gone Wrong	71
Heavenly Perspectives	73
Dreams Of Better Days	75
To Our Children	77
The Good Old Days	80
To The Old Folks At Home	85
I Stand In Awe	87
Man's Eternal Search	89
A Final Word	93
Acknowledgements	99
About John Saomes	101
Books By John Saomes	102

PREFACE

There is something very lovable about a true blue Aussie larrikin ... and Dinkumous J. Dodger is certainly one of the most loved. While he is an irreverent, opinionated, rabble-rousing prankster, Dinkumous is also genuine, down-to-earth, and the living embodiment of that rustic caring 'mateship' we've come to expect from a decent Australian bloke.

Most of the stories in this book are based on actual events and many of the colourful characters who feature in these poetic yarns are still living today. (You know who you are!) Of course, some of the names have been changed to protect the innocent ... and the guilty.

The early days of Dinkumous J. Dodger are light hearted, carefree, and comical. The humorous poems reflect memories of younger days set in rural Queensland during the sixties and seventies, garnished with a wealth of stories and yarns from previous generations. As Dinkumous matures and begins to understand the ways of the world, the poetry becomes more serious and contemplative, with impassioned pleas for political goodwill and candid reflections of a simpler time when there was less stress and political intervention in our daily lives — when people felt a sense of freedom and social harmony that encouraged them to live their lives in their own way and on their own terms. At the end of this book I've written a final word about the issues of that period, which helps to explain the background and setting for some of the more contentious themes.

Australian bush poetry as a poetic form is often rough and ready and quite different to the traditional works of the masters. Yet, when we allow ourselves to break free of pure poetic constraints and focus more on the message than the method, bush poetry provides a medium that is immensely flexible, giving the poet greater latitude for expression. The less than perfect rhythm and rhyme, together with the use of colloquial language peppered with Australian slang, can be more akin to yarn spinning than to polished poetic verse.

My purpose in writing this collection of poems is to capture that uniquely Australian brand of humour and irreverence that once set us apart from the rest of the world. In recent times, we've lost that dinkum Australian identity perpetuated by our forefathers who carved out a nation from a rugged, harsh land. The ability to win against impossible odds and a general disrespect for law and authority have shaped the wealth of characters and stories of our rich Australian heritage.

Some of the opinions expressed in Dodger's poetry are direct and quite pointed. The tone, opinions, and perspectives, of many of the poems candidly capture and reflect the mood in the bush through troubled times. Such opinions, as politically incorrect as they may be, belong to a particular section of Australian society and do not necessarily reflect those of the author. However, if you see something from a different perspective, or the content of this book gives rise to new thoughts or further discussion ... the Dodger would be pleased.

The days of the 'Aussie Battler' and all that such a phrase once engendered seems to have passed us by. Yet, these are the people who made us great as a nation. May they live forever in our memories, in our folklore, and in our poetry.

John Saomes

PART I

LAUGHING MATTERS

SCHOOL DAYS

"Why was ya late young Dodger?"
the ageing teacher asked.
"Tis very nearly smoko time!
Stand up and tell the class."

"Why was ya late young Dodger?
The second time this week!
And as it's only Tuesday,
should I give ya tail a tweak?"

"Or does ya have a good excuse
for why ya wasn't 'ere?
Pray, tell us boy. Where has ya been?
Speak up so all can hear!"

"Please Sir, well, it rained last night
and muddied up the track!
And every step I took uphill,
I slided two steps back!"

JOHN SAOMES

"For every uphill step I made,
I slided two steps down!
But then I got a bright idea!
I turned me'self around!"

"One step down made two steps up
and over the hill I came!"
The teacher pursed his wrinkled brow
and limbered up the cane!

Well Dodger had it coming.
He was never there on time.
And as the teacher swished his tail
he said this little rhyme.

"There's marks for 'magination
and exuberance of youth,
and marks for ingenuity,
but none for tellin' truth!

The idea of turning backwards to slide up over the hill came from an episode of 'Yes, What', an Australian radio comedy by Rex Dawe. The character Greenbottle is often late for class and this is one of his ingenious excuses. The radio series originally aired from 1936 to 1941.

OUTHOUSE BLUES

Dodger's Dad loved guavas.
He'd eaten quite a few!
A bout of diarrhoea
sent him out back to the loo!

He sat so long a storm blew in,
which added to his bother.
The wind came up in mighty gusts
and blew the dunny over!

It picked it up and spun it round
and crashed it down again,
and Dad was covered head to toe
with contents from the pan!

He scrambled from the wreckage,
and rubbed his eyes and blinked.
His head was spinning round and round,
and blimey did he stink!

JOHN SAOMES

Said Mum, "Can we get septic now?
Inside — warm and clean!"
But Dad was feeling stingy,
cantankerous and mean.

Next dawn Dad hitched the horse and cart,
with Dodger on his bike,
and headed off to go to town
to buy a brand new dyke!

About that time the sewerage scheme
was going through the town.
Dozens stood deserted.
You could buy one for a pound!

So Dodger chose a strong one.
He wanted it to last.
And Dad produced two ten bob notes
and then began the task.

They hauled it up the mango tree
and put the cart beneath,
and lowered it on and tied it off,
and headed down the street.

But halfway home Dad had to stop
to answer nature's call.
"Why don't you use the one on back?
They gave us can and all."

"Young man," he said. "I think I will.
There's fancy paper too!
I'd deem it quite a privilege
to christen our new loo!"

And meanwhile — Marmaduke the horse
was sniffing at the air.
He'd caught a scent that made him smile
from Farmer Johnson's mare!

And standing unattended,
he soon forgot his load,
and Marmaduke the lovesick fool
went prancing down the road!

Well Dad let out a bellow
and peeked around the door.
He thought young Dodger spooked the horse.
He'd give the lad 'what for'!

JOHN SAOMES

But there was Dodger close behind
and peddling for his all.
'Twas then they passed the Parson's wife,
and what a sight she saw!

Dad's trousers round his ankles
and the toilet door ajar!
She gasped "Oh Lord have mercy!",
and almost pranged her car!

The horse jumped to a canter
when the mare came into view.
The harness couldn't stand the strain
and kinda broke in two!

The Duke pulled free and bolted.
The cart slowed up — and then,
it started going backwards,
and down the hill again!

And Dodger turned his bike around
and peddled like the wind.
Dad screamed "Let me on with you
before we reach the bend!"

He leaped out for the bike — and missed!
Dodger gave a shriek!
The cart went through the barbed wire fence
and crashed into the creek!

And there was our new lavatory
floating in the drink.
The two sat on the creek bank
and watched it slowly sink!

Then doubling on the push-bike,
they went to find the horse.
The boy said "Dad, what will we do?"
"Put septic in of course!"

I remember a time when townships across Australia had an outhouse behind every home. Later, our backyards were dug up to install miles and miles of pipes, and the modern sewerage system came into being. Outhouses stood deserted by the thousands, and many farmers who were outside the sewerage scheme came to town to purchase a better outhouse while they were cheap and plentiful. Indeed, at one time, a pound was the going rate for a sturdy replacement. The relocation of said outhouse though, was never easy, and the source of many a disastrous and comical tale.

BAKING DAY

'Twas baking day for Dodger's Mum.
The best day of the week!
Fresh melon jam and nice hot bread
and lots of tasty treats!
The recipes for all of them
were written in her head!
But first the hardest task of all ...
Get Dodger out of bed!

"Wake up young man this minute
or I'll give ya ear a clip,
and out into the wood heap
and chop a pile of chips,
and then a pile of iron bark.
The splintery bits burn good.
And Dodger, please take extra care
and don't chop off ya foot!"

"We've had enough of accidents
around these parts of late.
Ya poor old aunty Mabel
caught her bunion in the gate!
And uncle Col ... It serves him right.
He came home late ... half full,
and went out in the moonlight
and tried to milk the bull!"

"And then ya Grandma ... Bless her,
all crippled up and old.
Mangoes fell on the outhouse roof
and scared her ... down the hole!"
And Dodger chuckled as he chopped
for 'twasn't quite the truth!
The lav' was 'neath the mango tree,
but Dodger dropped the fruit!

"And don't forget that's Grandad's axe,
so take some extra care.
Well, five new handles — two new heads ...
The sentiment's still there.
Then Dodger raised the axe on high
to get some extra thump.
He'd met with much resistance
from a twisted kinda lump.

JOHN SAOMES

He bought the axe down hard again,
then screamed out "Ah gawd strewth!"
The head came off the handle
and landed on the roof!
And on its way it managed
to chop the clothesline down,
and all their precious washing
had fallen on the ground!

He quickly tied the line back up
and dusted off the clothes.
Well most of them were clean enough
that Mum would never know!
But, Mum had heard the thunderous crash
and dropped a pot of stew,
and now screamed out the window,
"Dodger! ... What are you up to?"

"The head came off the axe ya see.
The handle's kinda bent.
I'll scramble up and fetch it down,
and stick it on again!"
But almost on the tankstand,
he yelled and screamed for Mum.
"My Darling, what's the matter?"
"I've a splinter in me bum!"

His mother burst out laughing,
which wasn't very kind.
She coulda showed some pity
for the pain in his behind!
The major operation
left it's mark on his left cheek.
But worse than that ... he found
he couldn't sit down for a week!

Oh the days when kids could climb up on the tank stand and onto the roof of the house! There was a sense of freedom then that no longer exists among our younger folk. We may have broken a few arms and legs jumping off, but it was good clean fun. To us it was all part of growing-up and learning to be sensible and responsible for our own actions. This concept has been largely taken from the younger generation by virtue of an inflexible system of laws, rules, and endless regulations.

THE CROOKED WILLY WONGLE

On the farm it's proper,
when men have need to pee,
they never use the thunderbox
but go behind a tree.

So all us country cousins
each evening could be seen,
shoulder to shoulder in a row
behind the mango tree.

And cousin Fred, in great relief
was shaking off the drops,
when Blue, that mongrel cattle dog,
bit his willy off!

Blood was spurting everywhere
and Freddy took a fit!
He thought he was a gonna
and the dog had eaten it!

Our close inspection seemed to show
that most of it remained,
though mauled and badly damaged
it would never be the same.

His Dad said "Now there's no one
to prolong the family name."
It was an awful tragedy.
His Mum said "What a shame!"

Well, what a raw predicament.
What was a bloke to do?
… And how would he conduct himself
when going to the loo?

We raced him off to hospital.
The nurses mourned for him.
They gave him royal treatment,
and sewed it on again!

They put a cast around it,
infections to prevent,
but when they took the plaster off,
the wretched thing was bent!

JOHN SAOMES

We all tried not to laugh at it.
Fred said, "Could be worse."
He said "I guess it's not so bad
as long as it still works!"

And work it does, as good as new,
but take a tip from me.
Never stand on Fred's left side
behind the mango tree!

THE PHANTOM BELL RINGER

A group of boys went chasing cats
and whacking toads with cricket bats.
And one was taken by the fact
that while they fainted from the whack,
cane toads rarely died from that.
They had more lives than any cat!

Years passed as years do.
The curious boy, now a troublesome youth,
developed a passion for devious plots
that got him in trouble quite a lot!
At times his pranks were not well received,
but his heart was good, as I'm sure you'll see.

JOHN SAOMES

The Sisters of Mercy at the Catholic School,
had prayed to God for a miracle.
And while he believed that wasn't wrong,
he thought he'd help the process along.
He'd stage an illusion that seemed to be
a divine manifestation for all to see.

The school bell hung in common sight,
and clearly seen in bright moonlight,
at midnight's chime began to toll!
The sisters startled to behold
that while the rope went up and down,
a bell-ringer could not be found!

"It's a miracle," they said
to others running from their beds,
and Sisters dropped upon a knee
and offered prayers of thou and thee,
and thanked the heavens for a sign
of blessed angels from on high!

The bell rang on into the night.
The local priest had thought he might
investigate the miracle,
and demonstrate to one and all
that faith in unseen things was good.
And keep the Sunday Service full!

But close inspection showed the chime
was driven by a more earthly kind.
For to the rope that made it ring
was a cane toad tied by a piece of string!
… And no one saw on yonder hill,
two chuckling youths who chuckle still!

DROUGHT IN BAMAGA

There's not much on in Bamaga
so locals hit the grog,
and nightly Constable Cleary
went on patrol with his dog.

Three cells were at the station.
He filled 'em all each day!
But locals didn't care too much
when Cleary put them away!

Half the folks who lived in town
had nowhere else to sleep!
The jail's the best repose around.
The rest had thought it a treat!

One day Cleary took a walk
down the end of the beach.
A crocodile grabbed his dog by the snout
and dragged him into the creek!

Cleary in fright ran all the way home
and got on the phone to Cairns;
instructed the zoo to send him up
a crocodile catching man!

The man arrived the very next day
and caught the monstrous croc,
but problems arose they hadn't foreseen.
'Twas far too big for the box!

Cleary said "Kill it! Don't take it alive!"
"What if the ropes should fail?"
The catcher said, "Till we build a cage,
Let's lock him in your jail!"

So while the locals went off to town,
their terrible tale to tell,
Cleary escorted the croc to jail
and gave him the middle cell!

That night the pub was deserted!
The frightened locals stayed home,
and all week long till the cage was made,
the town was as dry as a bone!

THE LEGEND OF THE ITCHING CRUTCH

University breeds pranksters.
It's always been that way.
Concentrated brilliance
is hard to keep at bay.
And we could spend forever
rehearsing all the schemes,
but one that Dodger prospered
was the best I've ever seen!

St. Ruth's, a ladies college,
where the country's finest stayed,
had gates that closed by half past ten
so staying out to play
was not permitted — NO EXCUSE.
The girls were locked in tight.
Security was tantamount
until that fateful night.

THE DAYS OF DINKUM DODGER - VOLUME I

A bunch of blokes went visiting
the ladies of St Ruth's
to take them to a disco,
though it wasn't quite the truth.
And Dodger went along that day
to pass some pleasant time,
and noticed all their underwear
was hanging on the line!

It seemed the laundry had closed down.
The workers were on strike.
A thousand pairs of panties
would be hanging out all night!
And Dodger's brain worked overtime
to come up with a plot,
to capitalise upon their plight
and desecrate the lot!

Then, he gathered us around him
to disclose his fiendish plan.
The fellas thought it brilliant.
They were with him to a man!
Now it would take precision
to execute with flair,
and quite a lot of risk involved
but no one seemed to care.

JOHN SAOMES

The night was dark. They jumped the fence
and crept around the side,
in combat mode like soldiers,
to the knickers on the line.
The jokers set about their task
with a maximum of care.
They brushed some itching powder
in the fork of every pair!

And when the deed was finally done
they bolted out of there,
and laughed about the quaint demise
of all the underwear.
They thought there'd be some scratching
and squirming in their chairs.
Perhaps a few would get a rash
but no one else would care!

But consequences of the trick
could scarcely be believed!
Several of the ladies thought
they'd caught a bed disease
and visited the clinic
and started naming names!
The reputation of St Ruth's
would never be the same!

Then parents heard the rumours
of goings-on at school,
and moved their precious daughters
to a more protective rule!
And other girls were punished,
and some were asked to leave.
They couldn't have their boarders
infected with disease!

And many a mother's guilty son
was panicking for sure.
The Priest who heard confession
was overworked and more!
And all the local gentlemen
whose secret had been kept,
had rushed off to the doctors
to line up for a test!

The pranksters, they were worried.
'Twas more than they had mused.
A couple of them even had
to line up in the queues,
and list their indiscretions
for at least the past six months,
results of which would not be good
for quite a while to come!

JOHN SAOMES

The final situation
was more than just an itch,
so when their secret surfaced,
they headed for the beach,
in case some of the casualties
had found out where they lived,
and set out to get even
for the wicked thing they did.

But time, the healer of most things,
had worked again for sure.
The humour of the exercise
was coming to the fore.
The pranksters became heroes;
well respected by their peers.
As stories circulated,
reputations grew with years.

And many a budding novice
has tried to top the score,
but the legend of the itching crutch
will live for evermore!

A TRUE IRISH ELEPHANT STORY

A hundred years ago or more,
in the Irish town of Tullamore,
an elephant fled from a travelling zoo
and made her escape as elephants do ...

When Paddy came down for breakfast one morn,
he saw the monster on Mick's back lawn;
and though his eyes were old and dim,
he couldn't believe what confronted him.

He looked and looked, and looked again.
'Twas all too much to comprehend;
so he telephoned his favourite neighbour,
thinking he might just do him a favour.

He said, "Now Mick - I don't want to scare ya,
but look out ya window. There's somethin' there ya
gotta see wit' ya very own eyes.
If I told ya — you'd say I was tellin' lies."

So Mick looked out but couldn't see
the weird looking monster under the tree.
"It's got around the side somehow.
He's in ya veggie garden now!"

"What's he doin' in there!" Mick wailed.
"He's pullin' carrots with his great big tail!"
"And what's he doin' with me carrots Pat?"
"Oh ... I can't begin to be tellin' ya that!"

According to one version of Irish history, the first elephant ever to set foot on Irish soil escaped from a travelling zoo near the town of Tullamore and was never seen again. This caused much consternation for the zookeeper as the elephant was his main drawcard, owing to the fact that the people of Ireland had never seen such a beast before ... Where the elephant ended up is anyone's guess, but a comical and colourful collection of misadventures such as the one recounted above continue to circulate through the annals of myth and legend to this very day.

BEFORE FITZGERALD

The party was a beauty.
The best in all the world!
Good food and drink and music,
and lots of gorgeous girls!
But all the lads had drawn a blank.
They couldn't believe their luck!
So off they went in search of fun
and landed in the muck!

The car was kinda crowded.
Eleven blokes in all!
Speeding down the highway
brought them trouble with the law!
With seatbelt fines and negligence
and going through a light,
suspected drunken driving,
they'd be there half the night!

JOHN SAOMES

The constable, a sternly man,
wouldn't overlook
the wrongs of uni students.
He'd hit them with the book!
But as he flicked the pages
and took the pen to write,
Dodger clambered from the car
to put the Coppa straight!

Said he "Can I suggest a way
for you to make a quid,
and save us all this paperwork?"
Then not a word was said!
The constable considered it.
He said "Now let me see;
the colour of ya money
and I'll let ya all go free!"
So Dodger sent around the hat
and emphasised the tale,
and urged us all "Dig extra deep
to keep us out of jail!"
So as they motored homeward,
they managed quite a smile;
but nothing like the policeman's grin!
'Twas broad as a country mile!

The Fitzgerald Inquiry into Queensland Police corruption (1987-1989) resulted in significant changes to Queensland's police culture and an enormous shift in the political landscape. Prior to the inquiry the long arm of the law was less intrusive, especially into the daily life of the regular bloke on the street. I'd even suggest it worked better than the over-regulated, inflexible, totalitarian regime of the current police service.

... And further — due to the potential legal and litigious aspects of this poem I will say no more than to attest to its absolute truthfulness!

KANTY'S HAT

Kanty was a country vet.
He had an aeroplane,
and Dodger from the D.P.I.
was pressing to explain,
about a mob of cattle
that were mustered in the yard,
and they could fly to there and back
and still be home by dark.

With Kanty's kind compliance,
he quickly climbed aboard,
but all the seats were taken out
so, sitting on the floor.
The take-off was as rough as hell
and Dodger had a hunch,
before the flight was over
he'd regurgitate his lunch!

The turbulence was terrible
and Dodger, feeling grim,
seized Kanty's fancy cowboy hat
and filled it to the brim!

Though landing was a great relief
he grimaced at the act,
and cursed at the concoction
that was soaking in the hat!

To Kanty, bouncing from his seat,
before a word was said,
he seized his fancy clobber
and flung it on his head!
He clambered through the tiny door
and leapt upon the ground,
which caused the brim to lose its load
and everything came down!

And from that day the visitors
from Regional D.P.I.,
could travel anywhere by road
but never in the sky!

D.P.I. — Department of Primary Industries

If my name was Michael G, I'd be very embarrassed about this one. In truth, the hat didn't quite make it onto the pilot's head ... but the rest is basically how it happened!

INSURANCE ASSURANCE

Dodger was a businessman.
Insurance was his game.
So Wilson's widow sought him out
to register a claim.
It seems her car was badly pranged.
She said she'd hit a roo;
but payouts from her policy
were not a brass razoo!

So Dodger offered some advice.
He urged her to concur
the truth behind the matter was
the kangaroo hit her!
He said, "The roo won't disagree.
The case will stand in court,
if you should swear your innocence
and someone else's fault!"

The widow's face looked guilty
and teary-eyed confessed,
"The kangaroo in question was
in fact already dead!
It lay beside the railway track,
a pile of stinking bones,
and somehow we'd collided
as I was driving home!"

So Dodger stroked his bearded chin
and squinted at the form.
The widow sat in silence
looking blankly at the wall.
Then finding her composure,
she gestured with a smile,
"If you could somehow fix it up,
I'll gladly pay you well!"

He grinned at widow Wilson's pluck.
She'd struck a common chord.
He'd surely work out something
to write upon the form!
And in return for services,
she'd eagerly agreed,
to place in his back pocket
a most substantial fee!

JOHN SAOMES

So, as we bear our burdens
and scratch each others' backs,
what goes around comes around
somewhere down the track.
Remember as you make your mark
or try to have a go,
It's not what you can do that counts
as much as who you know!

GOANNA STEW

Wun Long Dong was a Chinese cook
who learned his trade from a picture book.
He worked on a station out in the dust,
back when high interest was sending them bust.

Now Bossman Kelly opted to sell,
while grass was green and cattle were well,
to Yankie investors with pockets of dough,
and Kelly would stay on and manage the show.

But the Yank's ideas of how it was done
caused Boss to think him too long in the sun!
He swore at the owner and cursed the day
he'd signed his farm and future away.

So Wun Long thought he'd help Boss out.
He scratched his head and paced about,
and schemed a theory and plotted a way
to send Yank back to the U.S. of A.

That night round the table he served a treat,
the tenderest, tasty, most succulent meat.
The Yank hadn't tasted such vitals before,
and Yankee's wife had asked for more!

She petitioned cook for the name of the dish.
It looked like veal but tasted like fish.
Wun Long said "Missy, I make it for you.
Chinese grandfather call Goanna Stew!"

"I tell you my secret," he said with a wink.
"You hang him in gumtree till he start to stink!
Then add curry powder to take away smell,
and chop in pieces and boil him up well!"

The silence that followed was deafening at least,
while all of the stockmen continued to feast,
and compliment Dong on the beautiful meal,
and goanna steaks that looked like veal!

But Yankee Bossman began to turn blue!
His wife's face went purple. Her eyes bugged out too!
She ran from the table and into the yard,
and cursed the day they'd moved to the farm.

And all night long they took turns to be sick,
and didn't eat for the rest of the week,
and couldn't forget that horrible feast,
so they packed their bags and moved back east.

They left a note for Kelly to read,
... said "Do what you like. Send profits to me."
So Boss is happy and Wun Long too.
Their favourite meal is Goanna Stew!

Thank you to the people of St George, Queensland for this yarn.

SUNDAY MORNING FRACAS

Young Keith was in the S.E.S.
and they were on alert,
as Maurie and his family
were driving off to church.
And Keith pulled Maurie over
at the crossroads by the weir;
respectfully requesting that
he take a long detour.

The road was closed to traffic
and Keith had gestured so,
but Maurie waved a (two-fingered) gesture back
and told him where to go!
As Maurie drove around the sign
and hurried on his way,
Keith just smiled and shook his head,
but vowed to make him pay!

He sent good Sergeant Callaghan
to sit beside the track,
in patient, silent vigilance,
and booked him coming back!

S.E.S. — State Emergency Services

Many of the good people of Dalby, Queensland will know these characters and remember this incident, but no one laughed more than me!

By his own admission; if ever there was a bloke who should have been booked a thousand times over, it was Maurie! A nicer and a funnier bloke never lived.

May you rest in peace — ya ol' mongrel.

LURKS AND PERKS

Dodger's mate was a city vet
whose forte was fixing small household pets.
Toffee nosed clients were always impressed
when precious ones had convalesced.
The sweet little creatures looked better than new.
'Twas often the truth if they only knew!
Most of them came from the local petshop!
He flushed the old ones but still charged a lot!

He drove a fancy foreign car
from fees for swapping budgerigars!
But the sweetest income you could wish,
came from exchanging sickly goldfish!
His bedside manner was always keen.
He'd treat their pets like kings and queens,
and speak of injections and potions and pills,
and every suggestion increased the bill!

His reputation continues to soar
as satisfied customers hold him in awe.
The petshop owner won't say a word
or monthly sales might drop by a third!
But they're no worse than the medical quacks
who write prescriptions and hide the facts
that most of their patients could cure themselves
if they fixed their diet and exercised well.

Like ludicrous lawyers they feed on the weak
who aren't aware of the right things to eat.
An apple a day keeps the doctor away
and laughter is still the best medicine!

MY SALUTE TO DAD 'N DAVE

Dave was quite a dopey kid
They didn't have high hopes for 'im
His future sure was lookin' grim
'til Mabel came along

A willing, homely, country type
and though they thought her less than bright
and tried to keep her out a sight
she seemed to fit right in

And Mum, the matron matriarch
at times would yell and scream and bark
and often took them all to task
Stone the crows! Ya Drongos!

And then we come to dear old Dad
once a keen and lively lad
in later years was often sad
when everything went wrong

They settled on a dairy farm
amid Snake Gully's wondrous charm
It never did them any harm
to work from dawn 'til dark

Their time was of a tougher life
hard of luck and full of strife
They always tried to make it right
and did the best they could

There wasn't much those days to know
Life was good, and brief, and slow
They bravely took their highs and lows
and just got on with it

They summed up life in timeless prose
immortal words we all should know
"Weddin's may come 'n' weddin's may go
but milkin' goes on and on …"

'Dad and Dave' the radio series aired from 1932 to 1952 and was based on the 'On Our Selection' short stories by Steele Rudd. The original stories feature the antics of Dad and Dave and the folk of Snake Gully and shows 'life on the land' with optimism, courage and plenty of humour. These yarns, much appreciated by the public, went on to inspire the well-loved radio series, a stage play and various film and television adaptions.

PART II

LIFE & POLITICS

THE NOBLE ART OF RECITATION

FOR MILTON TAYLOR

Milton's mind — like matted wool
is filled with such compassion.
His gentle words caress the soul
and summon such emotion.

The feeling in his pleading fingers
melts the coldest frozen heart.
Imagination's images
express the purest
noblest art.

Milton Taylor (1943-2015) was a renowned and highly awarded Australian bush poet who influenced and enthralled all who heard him recite. Many of the poems in these volumes were inspired by his boundless love of Australia and the Australian way.

POLITICAL PERSUASION

The deathly silence whispers
out along the track,
where savage desert's beauty
greets the great outback.
When sweltering sun is sinking
and moon is on the rise
and stars are clear as crystal
and air is crisp and light.
Where smell of rain on gidgee
stirs insects through the trees,
You're just as far from Canberra
as anyone could be.

Where ocean breezes whisper
out across the blue,
and subtle sounds of breaking waves
caress the rolling dunes,
and sand and surf and sunshine
are the measure of the day,

and man can rest in splendid bliss
and dream his life away.
Where perfect thoughts of mellowed minds
drift slowly out to sea,
You're just as far from Canberra
as anyone could be.

By shores of Burley-Griffin
'neath the shadow of the flag,
where public servants mill around
and prattle on and brag
about their pointless conquests
and whinge about their woes,
where power hungry peasants
strut in thousand dollar clothes,
where wealth of a once great nation
is squandered all away;
You're as far from real Australia
as anyone could say.

If every lie could be exposed
and we could understand
the secret combinations
that are ruining our land,
and see the foreign puppeteers
manipulate the strings
that cause our politicians

to jump and dance and sing;
We'd see that those who make the rules
that govern you and me
are just as far from Canberra
as anyone could be.

United Nations covenants
are written into law.
Our Foreign Affairs Department
is rotten to its core.
So while our Constitution
sits dusty on the shelf,
our farms and factories all go broke.
We lose our national wealth.
But we could solve the problem
by a vote to keep us free,
and take control of Canberra
to rule for you and me.

Over the last few decades Australia has increasingly been influenced by foreign manipulation. The legislators in Canberra, Australia's capital city, have entered us into international covenants that over-ride our national laws and governance and hence, Australians have lost many of their rights afforded us by the Bill of Rights 1689 and Magna Carta.

DARCY'S DAYBREAK

The magic mists of early morning
hide us like a rising cloud
and veil the day's bright dawning
like a phosphorescent shroud.
The sparkling leaves and glistening grass
shimmer at the sun's first rays.
The waking forest ousts the dark
to usher in another day.
The silhouettes of ghostly gums
like sentinels on high,
and birdsongs trill to crickets hum.
The forest now becomes alive.
The artist's sketch is hushed and still;
but all the seven senses fill.

Inspired by the beautiful Australian bush scenes painted by d'Arcy Doyle (1932–2001).

GOVERNMENT CONTROLS

The government gag is circulating
Fining those discriminating
While the fools are legislating
Hear our silent demonstrating

The government goons are daily chiding
Banning fun like ute-back riding
Essential services are lacking
Youth escape who need a thrashing

The government lice are causing welts
forcing folk to wear seat belts
The government nerds are cursing kids
forced to wearing bicycle lids

The government fiends are waving hands
auctioning off our sovereign land
The ruling criminals in government facilities
are selling off our national utilities
The government traitors are taking pleasure
in giving away our national treasures

What an absolute mess!
What an absolute farce!
Lets rid ourselves
of government controls ... and fast!

DANGEROUS GAMES

'Tis a dangerous game we play,
when challenging those in authority;
for he who holds power, wields that power,
even when in the minority …

The price of tyranny is death to the innocent,
and suffering to the common man.
Tyrannical governments oppress the people,
simply because they can …

THOUGHTS OF THE NIGHT

AS WE PITCHED OUR SWAGS BY THE ROADSIDE NEAR BARCALDINE, OUTBACK QUEENSLAND

Who will visit me tonight?
Will love chance to pass my way?
Will sleep find my pillowed head?
Will I to dream …
of joy … or pain?

Will death seek me out …
before the coming dawn?

Tomorrow knows my fate.
I'll know when I awake —
if I do.
And if I don't —
will I know that too?

LAND RIGHTS

God created it — long ago …
Aborigines inherited it — everyone knows …
The British conquered it — have no doubt …
Australians developed it — surely that counts …
Our allies defended it — Asians out …
Now we've sold it — where to now?

With history of such tremendous change,
how can anyone press a claim?
But let's not have an all-out brawl.
Draw the lines. There's space for all!

The introduction of Land Rights for Aborigines brought a very contentious period in Australia's history. Settlers who opened up and developed the land had it taken from them with the stroke of a political pen. From that point onwards, a deed of title had little meaning. Land can now be resumed by the Crown without question, which signalled the end of private ownership as we knew it.

THE LONG YARD OF ANTICIPATION

Its lonely in the long yard
for those who stay behind.
The days are slow and dreary,
preparing for the time
when man and mob will come again.
When man and beast will chance their wit.
The passionate hearts are matched again
with muscle, sinew, guts and grit.
The days of sweet anticipation
fade to dusk and rise again,
and comforts round the campfires
belie the hearts of men.
The long yard lies deserted now —
but yonder comes the galloping cloud.

THE WUZZLE'S TALE

Fuzzle Wuzzle was a dog.
Buzzle Duzzle was a frog.
This tale we'll call the Wuzzle's tale
begins with Fuzzle locked in jail.

The downfall of the puzzled Wuzzle
came when he removed his muzzle,
made a stand and sealed his fate
by speaking out against the State!

The law was penned in letters red.
This is simply what it said.
"Dogs lie down and never stand,
and only beg upon command."

This law said "Frogs stay in the cold
and only jump when they are told."
And Buzzle Duzzle kept the law
and bore the pains of being poor.

But Fuzzle Wuzzle dared to speak
of peoples' rights and wrongs and seek
to overturn oppressive law
and make the system fair for all.

So Buzzle frog went off to prison,
paid the Fuzzle dog a visit,
savoured his inspiring words
and jumped for joy at what he heard!

Such constitutes a broken law!
The Buzzle frog went free no more,
and all the public servant slaves
upheld the law and dug the graves.

They buried Fuzzle Wuzzle deep
and Buzzle Duzzle at his feet.
The unjust laws remained this time,
upheld by public servant crime.

The system's bound to stay that way
till other Wuzzles dare to say
the things that cause their hearts to pain.
Or do we dogs and frogs remain?

To all the spineless traitorous lice
on Canberra's streets like plagues of mice,
scurrying for glory and power —
Your criminal rule will soon be over.

For Fuzzle dogs will lift their legs
and Buzzle frogs jump on your heads.
And Duzzles overturn your laws.
And Wuzzles tails will wag once more.

Who are the Fuzzles and Buzzles?

They are the 'ordinary Australians' who made a stand against Canberra when it was actively taking away the basic rights of the people. I make specific reference to the Australia Act 1986 that eliminates all powers for the UK Parliament to legislate with effect in Australia. However, with the introduction of this Act, Australians lost recourse to the Bill of Rights 1689 which listed the basic rights and liberties our forefathers shed blood for.

WE NEED A FIRST AMENDMENT

Upon these pages was a poem
to my earthly mortal home.
'Australia Dying' was its name.
The censor's pen curtailed its fame.
They said I couldn't speak my mind
or have opinions of a kind
that contravene the written law
or I would land in jail for sure!

"Surely not" said I. "You jest!"
Surely opinions can be expressed
and I can think whatever I like.
It's kind of like the right to strike!

Surely discrimination is viewed
as people's rights to pick and choose.
Indiscriminates can't be allowed.
Not the other way around!

But no! It seems we've come that far!
We now resemble the U.S.S.R.!
We have lost our basic rights.
When will Big Brother turn out the lights?

I point out that not all discrimination is unfair or prejudicial. Australians live in a very complex environment where expressing an opinion or showing preference can be interpreted as an act of discrimination that may result in complaints to the Anti Discrimination Commission.

Reference to 'Australia Dying' in this poem relates to my concern that Australian employees and companies are not given preference for contracts and jobs within Australia. Unfortunately, such an action can be classed as discriminatory under current legislation. As a result there is less Australian industry, higher unemployment and we are a poorer, less independent nation with foreign interests taking the lion's share of profits and funnelling them out of the country.

ODE TO THE DUNSTANS

I wasn't healthy and everyone knew!
All could plainly see.
Too many years of executive stress
were catching up with me.

My body was ailing and fast wearing out.
My spirit was heavy, my heart contrite.
I needed a tonic for rejuvenation.
I needed a rest from the pressures of life.

I caught every bug, every cold, every flu.
And tired of doctors and potions and pills,
I sought out a 'natural therapist' person
to work out my problem and strengthen my will.

The cure was worse than I ever imagined!
Each day before breakfast, five 'k's I must swim,
then walking or jogging or physical labour,
to sweat out the toxins and make my waist thin!

JOHN SAOMES

So off to the farm for the good of my health;
I came to 'Cambooya' — a paradise found,
where small crops and cattle dotted the landscape.
A lush fertile valley — a quaint country town.

The folk were as warm as the sunshine in summer.
God's own disciples — the salt of the earth.
Their manner the same as my far distant family.
Their ways took me back to the place of my birth.

Barry was boss and a man among men,
who worked twice as hard as most of us might.
With Eunice beside him — his faithful companion,
and partner and princess — a good farmer's wife.

Craig had a job that all of us envied.
While we picked the veggies — rows upon rows,
He drove the tractor backwards and forwards,
to-ing and fro-ing — and picking his nose!

The sun beat down and sweat pored out
and muscles ached and backs grew strong,
and day by day the torture was healing.
I took my medicine all week long.

My hands were hardened and blistered and cut.
My legs were stiff. My feet were sore.
My back was aching. My shoulders were burned.
Rejuvenation was silent but sure.

Today I'm back to my hectic existence,
healthy and stronger than I've ever been.
In suit and tie I'm off to the office,
to sit at my desk with clients to see.

But often I think of the road to 'Cambooya',
to life on the farm — that labour of love,
of the sweet satisfaction of sweat on my brow
and the smell of the earth and the sun up above.

For a farmer's day is longer than most.
A farmer's way is harder than any,
but a farmer's pay is honest and righteous.
A farmer's blessings from Heaven are many.

How will He judge us who dwells on high?
How will he measure each soul by and by?
Perhaps our income won't rate a mention,
but good honest labours will qualify.

WHAT ARE YOU TEACHING OUR CHILDREN

What are you teaching our children at school?
Why are you failing and turning out fools
with no sense of reason or purpose in life,
who don't even know how to read or write?

And where's all the money going to
that's allocated for teaching our youth?
It's not being spent in classrooms for sure,
which makes me suspicious. I want to know more!

And what's all this human relationships guff
that speaks of values and morals and stuff?
It seems the focus on sex and drugs
has increased the number of pushers and thugs!

And what of gender equity?
And why such a focus on birds and bees
to very young children who couldn't care less?
No wonder they show early signs of stress!

This social justice seems anything but!
Can't we decide to take potluck
or choose who we like to our personal taste,
irrespective of gender or colour or race?

When I was young, we knew where we stood.
The lines were drawn and the system was good.
Now there's confusion in children's minds
that wasn't there in previous times.

Three 'R's were taught throughout the land
and all could read and understand
the facts before them and know how to choose,
and parents were honoured, respected — not sued!

The right to choose remains the key
to building a world that's peaceful and free.
With codes of honour and chivalry
and a sense of purpose for all.

So teach our children to read and write.
Don't show the world in a socialist light.
Teach them facts and nothing more.
That's what education is for!

The concerns expressed in this poem stemmed from the 1990 ratification by Australia of an international document known as the Convention on the Rights of the Child, issued by the United Nations. It resulted in uncalled for changes to the school curriculum and an array of rights for children that many Australian parents did not agree with. Some of the Convention's articles were contrary to our way of life and parents were outraged that the Government was dictating how they should raise their children.

The other glaring problem is the amount of indoctrination encapsulated in the school curriculum. Many parents are concerned our children are being indoctrinated to accept all manner of socialist and humanist ideals and a range of behaviours that were traditionally deemed socially unacceptable or inappropriate, such as homosexuality, sexual relations outside of marriage, the use of drugs to change behaviour, and the steady erosion of respect for authority figures, including parents, teachers, and the elderly.

WORLD GONE WRONG

A criminal paces the polished floor.
There's bars on the windows and bars on the doors.
He's trying to come to terms with the time
he's sentenced to serve for committing the crime;
and dreams of the day when he will be free
to visit his friends wherever they be,
and carry on without a care,
with so much to do and so much to share.

An elderly widower stares at the floor.
There's bars on the windows and bars on the doors.
He's trying to come to terms with his life;
to reason the cause of the infinite strife
that poisoned his thinking and tortured his mind,
and wishes he were somehow blind
and couldn't see the world out there,
with so much to fear and no one to care.

JOHN SAOMES

But when you compare the money spent
on a criminal, and an elderly gent
who never committed a wrong in his life;
something doesn't seem to be right.
Ten times the amount is spent each year
on those who've done wrong and caused all the fear,
that keep the innocent frightened at night,
while crims go free to do as they like.

The world's no longer a pleasant place.
There's too much violence. It's too hard to face
the ugly, twisted and terrible scenes.
There's too much danger and too many mean
and ruthless and bloodthirsty men
who struggle for power. And we can't defend
our families, or make them aware
as situations develop out there.

So those who always abide by the law
have bars on their windows and bars on their doors.
They keep their distance and stay out of sight
and seldom go out by day or night,
but hide away in constant fear
and no one sees their silent tears.
The criminal's sentence expires in time.
The innocent ones are locked up for life.

HEAVENLY PERSPECTIVES

At times I can't but wonder why
nations starve and children die.
And men fight wars and kill and maim.
And no one knows just who to blame.
Who pulls the strings? Who makes the plans?
Who sets the course of life for man?

Surely mortal men cannot
be so puffed up and arrogant
to think that they might choose for all,
for every earthly kingdom falls.
For all the wisdom of the wise
will come to nought unless we rise
above the carnal, sensual beast
and selfish pride and lust defeat.

JOHN SAOMES

The power hungry moneymen
have sought to dictate where and when
the people of the earth would rise
and who would live and who would die.
And as they plot and manipulate,
I contemplate their personal fate.

For surely all will one day stand
the judgment meted out to man
for all their earthly works performed,
and some rejoice while others mourn,
and certain justice winning through,
and mercy for the righteous few.

DREAMS OF BETTER DAYS

Where are the men who made us great,
who kept us free from guilt and hate,
whose efforts we appreciate?
The champions of valiant crusades.

Where are the statesmen who made us strong?
I can't believe they've all gone.
Surely their blood is flowing on
and the spirit of righteousness lives.

Where are the virtues we valued back then?
Well-mannered ladies, courteous young men.
Could we hold such virtues again?
Surely we can if we want to.

Whom of us remember the day
when gentlemen's honour and courage were praised,
and proper young ladies were pure and chaste,
and sins of the flesh were scorned?

JOHN SAOMES

Where's the commitment 'tween husband and wife?
The determined resolve for the rest of their life
to honour and cherish and love and delight
and labour and toil for their children?

Surely the world is poorer today
as new age doctrines have led us astray.
The New World Order has taken away
all the freedoms our forefathers fought for.

Why can't we establish a system of law
where nobody suffers from famine or war
and democracy rules in it's simplest form
and we can live long and be happy?

With separate states for every race
and all the groups communicate
and judgement fair in every case
and everyone free to choose.

With all our human rights returned
and all the propaganda burned
and all the worthwhile lessons learned
and never to be forgotten.

TO OUR CHILDREN

Mum and Dad are always near,
from early days to ageing years.
So please remember — always know,
that till we're buried deep below,
our thoughts will always be of you.
You're our concern our whole life through.

And even when we pass beyond,
We'll look below with feelings fond,
and through the years that we're divided,
till we're once again united,
bonds forged in mortality
will bind us through eternity.

JOHN SAOMES

Our family — special, precious, dear,
every member year by year
making life's sweet poetry,
etching priceless memories,
giving purpose to our time
as parents in this mortal clime.
Helping each of us to grow
as onward to perfection go.

Life's lessons are the hardest learned,
through generations — death and birth.
The cycle ever rolling on
and children — parents soon become.

When you have children of your own
who tie their shoes and think they're grown,
spare a thought for Mum and me.
Remember well life's tragedy,
that children think that they know best
and seldom listen to the rest
of those who care so much for them;
whose wisdom youth will oft condemn,
in favour of the modern way,
and from the proven path will stray
until they learn to know themselves
of fleeting fads and timeless wealth.

Their lives for them we cannot live
and only love and guidance give,
in times when teaching moments come.
And pray for them to God above
that they might choose the better way
and hold to truth and never stray.

Yet as they fall and clamber up
and fail and drink the bitter cup,
each earthly trial, each trite concern,
each stumbling step's a lesson learned.
In time they're only memories
of our eternal family.

THE GOOD OLD DAYS

I wonder what my Gran would say,
of things that women have today,
that never used to be that way
when Grandma kept her house?

Modern gadgets have a knob.
You turn them on; you turn them off,
and sit back down and just … look on
while they do all the work!

No chopping chips. No wood piled high.
No washing hanging on the line.
No pigs to feed out in the sty.
The garbage truck comes Wednesdays!

We don't have plagues of rats or mice.
We don't have chooks. They don't have lice.
The automatic things are nice.
So what's to do all day?

THE DAYS OF DINKUM DODGER - VOLUME I

No pot-sticks, coppers, fires or blue.
No flat irons, lanterns, millet brooms.
Now women all grow fat — it's true,
from watching television!

I know Gran is not impressed
when modern women need a rest!
They wouldn't pass the simplest test
of things my Grandma learned!

Now I don't mean to point or gloat,
but men kept politics afloat,
until the women got the vote.
And now look where we are!

They used to keep themselves at home.
But now they have the right to roam,
and speak of men like garden gnomes
when off at coffee mornings!

The modern woman goes to gym
to keep her body taut and trim.
They've lots of time to … fill in,
while gadgets do their chores!

JOHN SAOMES

And what of all the men at work?
A duty they would never shirk,
to pay for women's lurks and perks!
We slave from dawn till dusk!

But what would Grandad say of me
with secretary on my knee,
and charging most expensive fees
when clients need advice?

And when the sun sinks in the west,
I think that I deserve a rest.
I sit behind a great big desk,
and push a heavy pen!

It's not quite what my Grandad done.
He worked in sweat and rain and sun.
Well like the women, we've changed some.
But not as much as them.

We're prone to dying young, we blokes;
from burn-out, ulcers, stress and strokes.
The pressure now's beyond a joke!
The old folks lived forever.

The oldies used to work all day,
and Sat'day night they'd earned their pay,
and got spruced up and off to play,
and dance and sing and laugh!

But most of us are all worn out.
So many worries to think about.
And seldom ever going out.
We can't afford it now!

So what say you to modern ways,
and modern cons of latter days?
My Gran was often heard to say
the best is yet to come!

But as I lay me down at night,
and contemplate our modern plight;
I wonder if it's wrong or right
that the 'good old days' are gone?

I'm hoping I don't get clobbered with a frying pan for some of the comments in this one. I wrote this poem as a 'tongue in cheek' look at life in the nineteen-eighties and nineties. My intention was to capture life as it was

for many back then and to point out how times had changed over the past few generations, especially for women.

We've moved on since that time. The next generation experiences new and different conditions at work and home. While I acknowledge some aspects have improved, I continue to question whether we're ultimately heading in the right direction, towards a better society.

What do you think?

TO THE OLD FOLKS AT HOME

When I was a boy we didn't have things
the young take for granted today.
I suppose it was harder, but we never noticed.
We happily went on our way.

In grasshopper plagues they circled the hut
with rings of smoking, smouldering coals.
That kept out the most — they still ate the soap,
and filled all the curtains with holes!

When the bushfires came they tied a few bags
to strong young saplings with pieces of wire;
and Mum kept them soaked, while Dad nearly choked
on the ashes and cinders and smoke from the fire.

JOHN SAOMES

In rat plagues they sat up all night with the broom
so we weren't bitten and dashed with disease.
And many a night they saw the dawn's light
while nursing our troubles and giving relief.

They patched up our bruises and boils and bumps,
our toothaches and heartaches they soothed away.
They always knew just what to do,
no matter what troubles would venture our way.

I STAND IN AWE

ANZAC TRIBUTE

I stand in awe of courage;
of those who raised their hand,
to 'heed the call — enlist to fight'
for King and motherland.

I stand in awe of bravery;
from boat to landing barge,
to beach — to hill — to battlefield,
at bugle's roar they charged.

I stand in awe of mateship;
that dinkum Aussie toss.
They stood with Kiwi brothers,
beneath the Southern Cross.

JOHN SAOMES

I stand in awe of loved ones;
who kept the home fires bright,
who worked the farms and factories,
and prayed them safe each night.

I stand in awe of national pride;
that fills the hearts of men.
Each year beneath the flag we bow,
in awe — remembering.

We cannot know — we cannot feel,
the suffering they endured;
the pain, the hope, the sadness,
the loneliness and fear.

They fought a fight for freedom
… the noble call to war,
and sacrificed for you and I.
Salute, and stand in awe.

MAN'S ETERNAL SEARCH

"Who is God?" a young man said.
"Is he someone old and dead;
whose course has run full circle round,
whose purpose now cannot be found?"

"And is there more than death and birth,
and good and bad, and is it worth
the time and effort we must spend
to seek for truth, to comprehend
the differences between the two,
of love and hate 'tween me and you,
of what to reap and what to sow,
of whence we came and where we go?"

"And what should man's great purpose be,
and how long is eternity?
What answers should I hunger for?
What questions should I ask? … and more."

Then came the sweet succinct reply.
"God is your father from on high.
Your mortal eyes cannot behold
the mechanisms he controls."

"Your body from the earth he made.
Immortal spirits from Heaven came,
born of heavenly parents there,
in perfect circumstances reared."

"Then spirit and body became new life.
You came to learn of wrong and right.
So here in lesser mansions dwell,
to appreciate Heaven and experience Hell."

"Your body to the earth returns,
while spirits crave for home and yearn
for all the things we had up there,
and searches — often in despair,
the better place for man to be.
It's not on land. It's not on sea,
but still our search continues on
until our mortal life is gone."

"But if our search leads us to know
that we could build down here below,
a piece of Heaven here on earth,
then what could be of greater worth?"

A FINAL WORD

This book of yarns and poetry was written in the early 1990's when life in Australia was very different than it is today. The political content of many of these poems registers the thoughts and feelings of a wide cross-section of Australians who were appalled at what was happening at that time.

    Now, a generation later, it is evident that Australia has undergone massive change over the past few decades that was politically engineered and not the will of the people. I and many others believe most of these changes are for the worse — and certainly not for our general betterment as a nation. By my reckoning, we are no longer the lucky country and definitely not the wealthy or self-reliant land we once were. Instead, we have become a crippled continent, subject to international markets, influenced by foreign powers, and governed from afar -- unnecessarily conforming to a host of international covenants, treaties and conventions that have led to the loss of our 'True Blue Aussie' identity and all that such a phrase once engendered. Without consultation or a vote of the people, Australians were forced to embrace the socialist ideal of multiculturalism and magically became part of Asia rather than remaining a separate and proudly independent land. We have ceased to be a nation anchored to Christian values, and many of our traditional links to Britain and British justice have been taken from us, along with all of our inherited civil rights. The rights and freedoms which our forefathers fought for over many generations were suddenly severed with a few strokes of the political pen — and most Australians do not know or realise this happened before their very eyes.

One such stroke saw the ratification of The Australia Act of 1986. While eliminating the United Kingdom's right to legislate for Australia, this sinister piece of legislation also removed our recourse to a thousand years of rights and privileges as members of the British Empire, including the principles of Magna Carta and the Bill of Rights of 1689. To this day, Australians do not have a Bill of Rights and remain subject to the rule of politicians and political will.

Policy changes have been surreptitiously implemented by Australian Labour, Australian Labor and successive Liberal Governments. The socialist doctrines of such groups as the International Labor Movement and The Fabian Society have slowly and subtly changed the 'Australian way', and continue to influence current policy. We have witnessed a huge step away from our democratic heritage as outlined in The Australian Constitution, towards Social Democracy, also known as Democratic Socialism. As a political ideology Democratic Socialism, where the people elect members of political parties to rule over them rather than representatives who independently represent the best interests of their electorates is sweeping the world, proposing ongoing reform and gradualist methods to establish socialistic systems and values globally.

These adopted socialist ideals led the Australian government to support the Lima Declaration, a set of agreements which later formed the basis of the United Nations Industrial Development Organisation. The outcome of this support saw Australian industry being dismantled in favour of Asian imports, and relocation of domestic manufacturing off-shore to bolster third world economies at the expense of our own. Over ninety percent of Australia's manufacturing has now been destroyed by this devious government policy, along with thousands of associated skills and jobs.

In addition, a significant amount of Australia — land and rural properties, commercial and residential real estate and businesses — is now foreign-owned. With assistance and incentives from the Australian Government and the banking sector, huge chunks of Australia have been sold to overseas interests under the banner of boosting foreign investment. This has happened to such a degree that Australia has been reduced to little more than an Asian outpost, to be used and controlled by people of any nation who have the money to buy a piece of it.

The protest poems contained in this book are my attempt to expose the secret agendas in Canberra and around the world, to be a voice of warning to those who are unaware of what is secretly happening, and to promote conversation; to get people talking and asking questions — especially of our politicians. As a proud Australian with six generations of heritage, I am appalled by what has taken place right under our noses. The country our children will inherit is destined to be a lesser place than previous generations have enjoyed unless we collectively speak out and make all Australians aware of what is happening, and use our vote to return Australia to the 'lucky country' it once was, while we still can.

ACKNOWLEDGEMENTS

Over 20 years ago I began to write Australian bush poetry. All my ramblings were saved by my 'state of the art' computer onto an old floppy disk. This single disk remained safely stashed in an old box which was lugged around the length and breadth of Queensland for several decades.

One day, almost by accident, I found the old floppy disk and decided to take a look at those almost forgotten poems — but despite many attempts, I couldn't find a floppy drive to read the old files. Corrupt code and error messages abounded ... Eventually I resigned myself to the thought that all was lost.

Then, without a word or even a hint, my wonderful wife found a data retrieval company that untangled and rescued two books of Dinkumous J. Dodger's poems along with three other volumes of modern poetry. What a wonderful surprise on my birthday! Dinkumous

J. Dodger was resurrected from the ashes of defunct technology. Thank you, Peta, for a most wonderful gift.

Of course, none of this poetry could have been written if not for all the inspiring Aussies I've met along the way. I pay tribute to those colourful characters who made life more interesting and enjoyable because of their 'dinkum Aussie larrikinism'. But, I'm not about to thank the politicians for providing me with such a plethora of material, because they've made such a mess of governing Australia, and forgotten that they're supposed to represent the people who elect them rather than votong along party lines -- which is unconstitutional and contrary to our democratic intent. (Just having my say, and so should you.)

I fully understand why the good people at Inspire Point Publishing took such a big gulp when they came across some of my more opinionated poems. However, they must have seen something worthwhile in them because they've agreed to publish most of them … although they're saving the most contentious for Volumes II and III. I thank them for their professionalism, and for sending my poetry out into the world in such a polished and presentable manner.

ABOUT JOHN SAOMES

John Saomes is an Australian poet and author whose books and novels follow the central theme of 'making the world a better place'. His writing promotes thought and discussion about the kind of world we desire, with emphasis on maximising happiness and enhancing the human experience.

John currently resides in the beautiful hinterland of Australia's Gold Coast and champions global initiatives to promote and uphold personal rights and freedoms, and efforts to build a better and fairer world for all.

You can contact John Saomes at:

www.johnsaomes.com

BOOKS BY JOHN SAOMES

From the Yuwmahn Compendium
Journey to Yuwmah
Ten Yuwmahn Beginnings

Poetry
The Days of Dinkum Dodger – Volume I

UPCOMING BOOKS BY JOHN SAOMES

From the Yuwmahn Compendium
Return to Yuwmah
The Yuwmahn Manifesto

Poetry
The Days of Dinkum Dodger – Volume II
The Days of Dinkum Dodger – Volume III
Beneath an Alphabet Moon

www.ingramcontent.com/pod-product-compliance
Lightning Source LLC
Chambersburg PA
CBHW020619300426
44113CB00007B/714